Everything Neon

POEMS

Bud Smith

MARGINALIA PUBLISHING
NORTH HOLLYWOOD, CALIFORNIA

Marginalia Publishing
North Hollywood, CA 91601
marginaliapublishing.com

EVERYTHING NEON. Copyright ©2014 by Bud Smith

All rights reserved. No part of this book may
be reproduced except in the case of short
quotes for use in reviews or literary analysis.

The following poems have appeared previously, some in slightly different form: "A Crushed Pepsi Can Floats Down" in *Olentangy Review*, "Where You Were Dead" in *The Nervous Breakdown*, "Love In the War Zones of the Wild" in *Citizens for Decent Literature*, "An Illustrated Book of American Songbirds" in *Full of Crow*, "You Can Remain Anonymous" in *Thunderclap!*, "Fire Escape" in *Clutching at Straws*, "Ping Pong" in *Zygote In My Coffee*, "Levitation Ring" in *Santa Fe Literary Review*, "Cool Hand Luke" in *The Idiom Magazine*.

Edited by Heather Dorn and Robert Vaughan
Cover design by Rae Buleri
Interior design by Rae Buleri and Allan Ferguson

ISBN 978-0615980782

FIRST EDITION, MARCH 2014

8/2/15

M'F'n
Indiana

---
for Spout

Bud Smith

Notice

NO BALL PLAYING

NO CARRIAGES

NO PEDDLING

NO LOITERING

NO DOMINOES

NO SITTING IN FRONT OF
THE BUILDING

—THE MANAGEMENT

You Can Remain Anonymous — 1
Levitation Ring — 5
A Crushed Pepsi Can Floats Down — 7
Street Parking — 8
They Pay Us on Wednesday,
But Now It's Thursday — 11
On My Way — 13
We Were Never Here — 14
Saturday Morning — 16
Not Enough Cream and Sugar
for the Both of Us — 18
Love in the War Zones of the Wild — 19
In My Building — 21
12 and ½ — 26
Pre-War — 28
Nothing On — 29
Fire Escape — 30
Orange Light — 32
I Kiss My Wife — 33
Anything and Anything — 34
The White Light Bridge — 35
Just Some Things You Say — 39
We Collect Skulls — 41
Dead — 43
If the Fire Is Not in Your Apartment — 44
Waves + Air — 46
Left-handed Scissors — 47
Lightning Box — 49
Youth — 51
Where You Were Dead — 52

Nights Underground — 54
Curfew — 56
It Snows — 58
Not Leaving — 61
Sidewalk — 65
May 4th — 66
The Yellow Table — 68
P.O. Box — 69
I'm from Electric Peak, MT — 70
31 Minutes — 72
An Illustrated Book of American Songbirds — 74
Other Birds — 77
Takeout — 80
Spring — 81
Talking to People You'll Never See Again at Parties — 82
A Cool Fictional Character — 83
Summer — 84
Swimmers — 86
Purple Gel Tab — 87
Sonny and Cher Sing "I Got You Babe" — 89
Low Light — 90
Music — 91
Nilsson — 92
Other People's Mail — 93
Not in Service — 95
Wife — 96
Extra Ladder — 97
Making Out — 99
Effective — 101
Taxi — 103
You Do Great Good — 107
Too Much — 108
To Succeed — 110
These Things Take Time — 111
All the Perfect Music — 113

Exact Sciences	115
Antitoxin	116
Third Rail Alive	117
Your Changes Have Been Saved	118
Opera	120
Keys	121
Between Liftoffs	122
Ordinary War	124
Stereo Up	125
I Like Your Shoes	126
Reaction	128
Don't Worry	129
Not an Accident	131
Spout	132
By a Fire	133
Defense Mechanism	134
Best Kind of Curse	135
Listening	137
Dominoes	139
Thanks for Making Me Feel Like Cool Hand Luke Today	141
Sing to Me	143
For My Friend Who's Still Alive	145
No Plans	146
True Believer	148
A Week	150
Off-Key	161
Love Song of the Insane	162
Edge	167

Everything Neon

You Can Remain Anonymous

from time to time
we descend the fire escape
declaring war on 173rd street

on Friday night
there was a wall of cops
on the corner
a girl was abducted
in an unmarked van
gunpoint, ski masks
children saw it all
crouching behind
the chain link fence
in the dog park

our problems:
the corner store is closed
we have to walk uphill to get beer
there's construction
they've torn up the road
I loop around forever
searching for a spot
"in the city it's not called a road"
"who fucking cares?"

the subway will soon contain
all the hellstorms of Hell itself
and we will sweat
the fruit-stands return
but nothing is ripe yet
I eat it anyway
like a world destroyer
nothing sadder than a bland pear

Saturday, a squad car
drives all up and down the block
blasting a looped statement
"if anyone has information
regarding an incident
involving a missing person
and a white unmarked van
driven away in the night
please contact the NYPD
you can remain anonymous"

for lunch I make eggs
I make bacon
the toast is perfect
best toast I've ever toasted
we sit at the yellow table
slowly sipping hot coffee
eyeing each other up
all while the cop cars
slowly circle below
playing that statement

she's afraid. I'm afraid
it's like we will be dragged off
at any moment
by our hair, by our teeth
by the veins of our heart
however they'd figure out
how to do that
criminal masterminds

Monday, at her desk
her co-workers ask her about it
"*the thing*" It gets much coverage
all across the office
by lunch, a girl has found some info
online that says: "over the weekend
persons of interest came forward
and confessed to police that
they were involved in the 'abduction'
on 173rd street. It seems
a young man was picking up
his girlfriend for a
SURPRISE BIRTHDAY PARTY
and startled her. she screamed
she got in the van. they drove away
to the party. had cake. had balloons
that was it. happy birthday"

and I stand
at my corner store window
peering into the darkness

wondering when we'll crash land
into Heaven, and get our just rewards
for all of our uphill struggles
never, probably
I crunch into a hard nectarine.

Levitation Ring

all afternoon there was thunder
but no rain came
we laid on our sides
facing each other other
eyes like tropical birds
ping-ponging through
a cave of shiny stone

there's a flash of lightning
there's a face, a road, a dream
I sell levitation rings for seven dollars
she floats in her sleep for free
I'm an optimist about Hell
I should be shot, she should be held
All the weathervanes do the twist
just like they did last summer

and our love spins in the crazy wind
as a fitted sheet, and a white t-shirt
are ripped off the laundry string
draped between pre-war buildings
and the thousand coats of paint fire escape

we're staring out the window
as the rain finally hits
the white shirt falling
the fitted sheet soaring
somehow, far beyond
173rd street.

A Crushed Pepsi Can Floats Down

your side of the world is flooded
mine is on fire
helicopters circle
dropping emptied juice boxes
candy bar wrappers
crusts from sub-par sandwiches
these days
even god has a day job
when I talk to people trying to live to 185
I get to thinking about dying
and coming back as a fish
the ocean is supposed to rise 25 feet
sometime, whenever
it was a frozen custard stand
engulfed in flame
took the boardwalk
Lucky Leo's
Carousel Arcade
use the fine reeds as a makeshift snorkel
tell the fire marshal I said hello
I'm building a raft from a neon sign
and will be there soon
made of bells.

Street Parking

I looked everywhere
still couldn't find my truck
there was nothing
between 176th
and 163rd
no sign of it
the river. the bridge.
the hydrants. the park.
me walking, one hand
in pocket, the other
clicking
a useless plastic
panic button
beer bottle popper
keychain
who would want
a forest green
1997 Ford Explorer?
what kinda sadistic fuck?
I stop on a bench
and watch a pigeon
then 3 white sweat-suited
women
doing tai chi

on frost covered grass
in the distance
a man in a brown leather coat
plays himself at chess
he keeps getting up
and walking around
to the other side
of the concrete board
considering his next move
on Broadway, I cave
first I call the cops
they say, "don't have it"
I call the tow lots
"we don't have it either"
it's gone to car Heaven
it's floating on a cloud
oil is still leaking down
like rain, secretly on everything
when I call the cops again
to report the thing jacked
long gone, stolen
chopped up, eaten
they say, "we got it"
"what?"
"it's on 177th
didn't you see the signs?"
"no"
"they were neon"
"everything is neon," I say
"they were filming a movie"

I walk over there
head down
birds suddenly singing
all trash levitating
the street sweeping machine
rounding the corner
and the driver shouting my name
there is my truck
on 177th
parked the wrong way
on a one way street
with a neon sign
that says: TOWED BY NYC POLICE
DO NOT TICKET
I climb inside
I turn the key
it shakes to life.

They Pay Us on Wednesday, But Now It's Thursday

sometimes yes
now, no
instead
lay horizontal
until all your fluids
ideas and juice
plus gravity
are carried off
somewhere else
where god herself
only knows
the dreams
of dreams
are getting close
our radiator whimpers
the sun flinches out
fire rolls through
the drive-thru
and who
are we to guess
our lives
are small
un-mechanical things

occasionally wounded
often folded
seldom to be melted
down to gold
I just got my paycheck
and it wasn't enough
now I'm going to sleep
see you there
in all your light.

On My Way

I'll swim down silver rivers
tiptoe across sleeping fields
and rest on the cliff
eating unguarded eagle eggs
big as a suitcase
before I climb
ivy rope vines
leading up the rockslide
mountainside
and find the ruby sword there
perfectly lilt up
in nefarious moonlight
they have my girl
in the fire catacombs
chained to a glowing wall
I'll throw a handful of ghost coins
onto the ground
stepping into the portal they open
as everything dissolves into purple smoke
I swallow a fistful of hearts
before I appear on the lava's edge.

We Were Never Here

say nothing to the others
fix ourselves, flat
against a brick wall
(do specified prequalified
miracles)
hold one's breath
for this lifetime, the next
and whatever is after that
WE   WERE   NEVER
      HERE
the names by the buzzer
remain from six lifetimes ago
tenants: guaranteed ghosts now
hover out in the shadows
in response, make a version of love
be fruitful in the bomb shelter
outside, find:
gumball machines vanished
pay phones on hiatus
empty streets and sidewalks
notices for the after-life
scotch taped to the P.O. box
saying:
ON MONDAY
FOR TEN HOURS, THERE WILL BE
NO WATER IN THE BUILDING

sigh loudly in your last shower
in the steamed up mirror
draw a map of the underground
then, back track, hail cabs
up Apocalypse Ave.
wear the pace train down
while disguising your steps
in wet concrete
hopping from curb to curb
flatten not a blade of grass
vanish one day
like all the other
neighbors
ghosts now.

Saturday Morning

while you slept
I was very still
in the pink room
in another world
and while you dreamt
I wrote sideways
with shaking hands
music like demolition
a record player wobbling
and a slow headache
working but waiting
for you to almost-wake
eyes like hummingbirds blink
and then I'll start
the ritual of coffee
and the worship
of bacon and eggs
amen
the gold and green
often come
crashing through
our brick wall home
when you call my name
I'll leave my desk

and come back to bed
setting our blankets
on fire.

Enough Cream and Sugar for the Both of Us

Saturday and heavy rain
Spout slept, facing the open window
I came into the room, sat on our bed
she gave an unconscious coo
the kind of thing a small bird does
I said her name three times
touching the nape of her neck
then I went to the yellow table, waiting
where I sipped hot coffee
"she'll be happy as fuck"
out the window
it was raining, as we'd hoped
I drank my coffee black
saving her cream
saving her sugar
a sacrifice made
to ward off evil spirits
from apartment 12.

Love in the War Zones of the Wild

when all else fails I will be good
no more flip flopping
dragging along, eating dust
dying slowly—pretending to like it
instead I will eat power pills
chew invincible bubblegum
I'll use fake coins, sign on dotted lines
to combat these problems:
ripped maps, traffic signs
"hope you slept well"
"no, I didn't sleep at all"
ignored a long time at every door
on every door, hang a sign
YOU WON'T KEEP ME OUT FOREVER
talk to anyone who'll listen
about: neon fish, strange darting birds
love in the war zones of the wild
telephone wounds, vinyl records
heaved at the moon—your father
and your mother and the field
where they'll be buried one day
but for now, practice doing donuts
in the parking lots of Hell,
underneath busted streetlights

find lost tickets, getting notices in the mail
snail mail, memos from long lost prom dates
send yourself a letter while drunk
receive it two days later, sober
the letter says, "I'm so thankful
for your love and correspondence"
how I met you: you in the rain, looking good
me in the mud, looking at you
high fives with the wind; kissing blues
kissing stones, kissing anything that moves
looking, listening, constantly revising
and then you leaned down
where your lips touched me
I can still feel it pleasantly stinging.

In My Building

in my building there's a white woman
who comes up and knocks on my door
every time I slam the refrigerator too hard
she says she is troubled by the noise
not just my noise, all the noise
I ask her, "Have you heard the little boy
who plays the drum set in 14B?"
"no," she says, horrified
I just shrug, she swivels on the balls of her feet
and goes away,
until the next time I have to close
the refrigerator door

in my building there's a little boy
who plays the drums
he didn't used to be so good
but he's getting better
it's hard to get good
at a full drum kit in the city
someone's always trying to stop him
no one wants to tell this little boy to stop
his father—the manager
is a 300 pound bulldozer
just released from prison

the boy's backing band
consists of three pit bulls
one on lead guitar, one on the bass
the final one on rhythm
none of the dogs sing
their vocal chords have been removed
they're just waiting patiently
for the police to show up
and raid the place
so am I

in my building there's a cat
that walks across a piano
I can hear it up there sometimes
stepping across randoms keys
mostly the notes make no sense
occasionally, a few will string together
and I'll quietly feel my heart break
while I lay in the darkness below

in my building, everyone puts in
air conditioning window boxes
after spring, except for me
I keep my window open
and just sweat
I look down on the street
and green leaves below
and listen to the Dominicans
playing baseball on the basketball court

I listen to the girls talking loudly
on the sidewalk, thinking they're
out of earshot and that everyone
is locked away till the summer burns itself out
I listen to the water run down the storm drain
from the open fire hydrant, and I listen to the
woman down at our trash cans
separating the glass bottles
piling them all into one shopping cart
that seems to be as big as our lives

in my building there's a couple
that fucks each other into oblivion
we can hear them through the pipes
but can't figure out where they are
who they are, if they're even
in the same dimension as us
we study the strange faces
as we pass in the hallway, waving
we study envelopes
when we get other people's mail
for some clue, any kind of forensics
about the people fucking each other
into oblivion through the pipes
it could be any one of us

in my building there's a person
who leaves their old magazines
in the gold paint foyer
on the radiator by the front door

they're lousy magazines
but I always look through them
I'm always ready to find something
I always find nothing

sometimes, I can just open
up the window and say, "heads up"
and the woman at the trash cans
catches my empty beer bottles
placing them lovingly in her shopping cart
it saves us both the effort
sometimes, I think about the cat
walking across the ivories
and pretend it's a beautiful naked woman
at the piano bench

sometimes, I think about dragging
my Moog synth across the hallway
and joining the band of pit bulls
and the 300 pound ex-convict and the little kid
owning those drums

sometimes we pretend that we're the couple
that we hear through the pipes and send the
noise right back at them into the pipes
hoping they are as bewildered as we are
it might be that what they do
is not because it's what they do

but because it's just a reaction
to what we do
have you ever considered this?

sometimes, I take the shitty magazines and give
them to a guy I work with
who has tropical birds, that he says
are ecstatic about shitting on *People* magazine
as opposed to say, the *New York Times*
I never ask him what kind of birds they are
tropical is good enough for me

and to be honest, sometimes, just sometimes,
I slam the refrigerator door on purpose,
extra hard, breaking the eggs
just to get *her* to come up here.

12 and ½

the Chinese food delivery kid is confused
we called in fried rice, egg rolls and soup
and it's been so long, I know
from experience
that he's standing
in the broken-tile hallway
staring at two doors
our door, apartment 12
and our neighbor's door, apartment 12
"you want us," I say
I'm holding the cash in my fist
he's gripping the plastic bag
with the cartons and the steam
and the free calendar for next year
he points to the doors
"12? and 12?"
"superstition, no one wants to be 13"
he nods but is still hesitant
he's not taking my money
and he's not passing the plastic bag
a woman walks up the stairs
with an empty birdcage
a man walks down the stairs

with trash juice leaking out
and I say, "alright, let's go"
the kid gives me my food
I give him the money
in Apartment 12
I place the bag on the yellow table
and take out the scissors
and the free calendar
and I cut out some letters
ransom-note-style
and walk back out into the hallway
I tape "½"
on the door
and inside, I can hear
my neighbor singing
he's in some kind of opera
he's superstitious
he's got a roommate with Tourette's
that I can hear sometimes
when I'm at my desk
I almost knock on their door
I come very very close
but in apartment 12
I can hear Spout call my name
as she pours the ginger ale.

Pre-War

upstairs
there's
the groan
of a television
furniture
rumbling
what must be
oranges tumbling
on the floor
rolling
all night long
in slow
revolutions
around the TV
as if it were the sun
beneath our
pre-war
building
there's a bomb shelter
where I go to read.

Nothing On

eventually
the static snow
on the TV
becomes birds
that fly
fearlessly
through waterfalls
and disappear
over our shoulders.

Fire Escape

out on the fire escape
watching the sun
about to crush
the adjacent building
…oh…
it didn't crush it
the sun was just setting
that gets me every time

looking across the street
at the rooftop
with purple holiday lights
that never
came down
and the girls smoking
they aren't sending me
smoke rings yet
but they will
if the wind changes

I'm making an itemized list
of everything
that I'm not going to do
for the rest of the night

and then
I'll be leaving
the notebook
with the list
inside the pigeon coops
while they go crazy
and coo
and my sneakers
sink so deep
into the hot magnetic tar
of the roof I'm not
allowed to be on
as/per: THE MANAGEMENT

there's a breeze up here
but the view is sobering

so

I go back in my window
and write another love letter
to somebody, anybody
in any of the lit up windows.

Orange Light

an orange light
appears in a window
I watch, amused
for awhile
till the bulb pops
and the dark comes back
then I watch the moon
change the glass
from blue, to white
to gold
it's better when I click off
my own orange light
I notice the shadow then
of someone/something
something/someone looking
in the vague direction
of either me
or the moon
from another darkened room
I wave, and nothing.

I Kiss My Wife

below the window
a car alarm goes off
the night could last forever
or end all at once
Spout rolls over
"no one owns that car"
"for sure"
the street and the sidewalk
have become something else
we don't leave the bed
laying there, we can see
the headlights coming on
and blinking off
shadows, reflections
patterned horns eternal
shrill metal squeals
we're just one window
of a thousand windows
looking down
on a shared riot
all of us: work in the morning
I kiss my wife, ignoring
the blinking lights.

Anything and Anything

at 1 AM
the car alarm stops
all on its own
no one came
nothing changed
and now the night
is released from amber
in between phases
of anything and anything.

The White Light Bridge

at the end of the street
is the white light bridge
one morning in the fog
I walked across it
people in cars sat in gridlock
not even singing aloud
with their stereos
a girl on a bicycle passed
at what felt like warp speed
horns rang out
a voice shouted, "move!"
the fog grew
I was out of work at the time
and in no great hurry
I stopped and watched
tug boats moving slow
on the silver river below us
I noticed the safety nets
for the jumpers
and thought about
trapeze artists, falling
after missing
mistimed handgrips
The White Light Bridge Circus

suspension lines, box trucks
lions, elbows hanging out, tailpipes
windshield wipers, elephants

in the middle
there's a sign that says
WELCOME TO NEW JERSEY
half the river, half the air
half the traffic, the fish below
cross this line at your own peril

I walked towards
a wall of black rock
and the park up top
an observation point, view glass
I fed a quarter into the mouth
to look into my
own apartment window
over there in the city
       empty
I'd have liked to see my wife
at our yellow table
drinking the last of the coffee

joggers run up the path
birds swoop from branches
a sailboat drifts south
out of place

on my way back
I run into the bridge cop
he was leaning on the railing
talking to himself
I wanted to ask
"wouldn't a jumper
just carry a box cutter
to sever the net?"
but I didn't interrupt
and he never looked up

passed the middle divide
the walk got easy
straight downhill
and then wrapping back around
traffic one way
footpath another
the horns diminished
into a level street
a row of green trees
red brick, fog becoming mist

on the sidewalk
I saw a leather wallet
sitting half-open
like an A-framed house

I picked it up
        empty
except for the note
taped inside

block letters:

"I'VE GOT MY EYE ON
 YOU"

I put the wallet down.

Just Some Things You Say

no more poems
about girls
who don't wear underwear
or waiting for a bus
that won't ever come
or winter
all day I thought
of a direct ride
to somewhere
other than here
I imagined
everlasting spring
and long-legged
deep-lunged girls
taking the stairs slowly
all the way past
purple clouds
spilling up
forever
I slept on a bed
of every book
I've ever read
shredded down
softer than heather

with my record player
at less than arm's length
and the radiator
chanting.

We Collect Skulls

expect to be famous
when no one is looking
sooner or later
you'll be shot through a cannon
into our loving arms

fair warning:
most of our heroes
get shot in the head

habits include:
quoting cult movies
getting fucked loudly on payday
dreaming with the fridge open

ever briefly
the garbage men and women
haul away our paperback dreams
as our all-knowing K-9s
whoof the lottery results:
verbatim

we collect skulls
we smash them on the floor
and spin the shards all night

we pile them so they lock together
like Legos and Lincoln Logs
painted jaws and Cro-Magnon teeth
I wonder who this one was

was it the guy who wrote my favorite song?
was it the girl from the billboards
in all my dreams?
was it the alligator tamer in the sewer?
was it long gone Brainyblonde?
was it Exemplar?
was it you?

I light the candles in the sockets
and study our phrenological charts
the maps of the underworld are drawn
by those who've traversed cloud city
with an open mind
and flattened teeth
now gripping figs.

Dead

probably not by machine gun
most likely nothing thermonuclear
light will just blink out, ordinary
a vinyl record ending
the automatic arm
returning to its plastic tab
probably not going to Heaven
probably not going to Hell
life is a weird rumor
somebody somewhere started
blue sky fatal
salt sea brutal
green fields
bisecting lifetimes of brick walls
there's a chance
my fossil will be mistaken
for something else
when opening seashells
check for IEDs
and pearls.

If the Fire Is Not in Your Apartment

if you get crushed in this city
that's your own problem
careful where you cross
we've hailed taxis through the lava
to traverse a cold street
occasionally stopping to dream
on benches or church steps
anywhere with shade

through the walls
I hear the opera stop
and down below
soon the hydrants will burst apart
check your palm on the door
the fire is not in your apartment
it's everywhere else

be forever patient
crawling through the smoke
your building was built
to withstand the bombings
but no planes dropped letters
the only mail you get
in your small P.O. box
are other people's bills

so leave
leave the perfect angels
in the radiators
leave the kingdom
of blue-ball mice in the walls
all thousand generations of them
leave the graffiti
of your neon-non-children
and your neighbor screaming
out the schedules
of alternate side
and third rail alive
in operatic tenor

slide through the tunnels
crossing beneath the water
come up in the swamps of New Jersey
you, a random tetrapod
looking for lost turnpike coins
in the slot between the seat
and the floorboard

the ocean, still rumored
lays ahead.

Waves + Air

on a good night
there's the waves
and air
of distant traffic
the sound of the moon
scraping across
the tips
of adjacent
buildings
and if I'm lucky
even my own.

Left-handed Scissors

items at my desk:
black wax skulls, golden eagle keys
framed photographs of bears
eating the tame animals
circling in for an endless sleep

thoughts:
it's okay to crash land you know
bubblegum pops
test pilots fall from clouds
like awkward rocks

prayers:
everything comes easy
because no one has to see
how much you bleed for it
s'all just pancake syrup
s'all just Dollar Store gadgets
wind-up whirly birds, left-handed scissors
Tokyo calculators, Ramen Noodle by the pallet

practices:
but—I don't disappear in a smoke screen
ducking through a doorway of moonlight

I found the chair I sit in unoccupied
because it's an ejector seat
my friends all used the same entrance
they come by unannounced, bringing debris
others couldn't stand to keep in their house
we assemble it all into a junk heap
building robot missiles
mounted on neon tetra castles
aiming at random into the maze of our lives

anecdote:
the other day someone asked
"what's wrong with society?"
I said, "society is full of too many people
who've never built their own roller-coaster."

Lightning Box

keep eating Chinese food
getting drunk, necking
prank phone calling radio stations
ringing doorbells—running

bite your winter-green mints
throwing sparks in the dark
stay young, stay feral, stay oblivious
get a car, burn up all the gas in the world
till there's no more gas or no more world
interrogate the girl sitting
alone in the laundromat
watching the machine spin
until she confides
"the secret to life is soap"
ask questions to the man at the bus stop
with the missing limbs
where did he leave them?
are they still there waiting?

intercept secret coded messages
slipped between full color junk mail glossies

decode it all—get back to me
tell me what it means
I'm distracted by the Cheez-its,
the Cheetos, the steak dinner prizes
whispered on the wind

keep calm, keep hope
keep a list of times, places and dates
keep annual receipts, keep quotes
keep photocopied printouts
of all the gemstones, all the flowers
all the instances of anatomy
—and how they've occurred
between you and me

send money, send love, great heights
settle in, smash bricks, dream right
keep saving marshmallows for last
enjoy them after the cereal
or if you wanna live right
eat the marshmallows, fuck the cereal.

Youth

when we were little
our mutual dream
was to slam dunk
so hard
we'd shatter
the glass backboard
that was it
our whole dream
and now
here we are.

ere You Were Dead

I remember rocks hitting teeth
and punching a kid in the mouth
the way he bled on his white shirt
that said, "Dino the Last Dinosaur"

there were trips to the beach
we dug down so far the ocean showed
my brother and me in the pit we made
under a violent sky, drawn sloppy
with blueberry scented markers

I dare you to live forever, I'll do the same
punch buggy yellow, punch buggy green

then we walked through the tunnels
armed with tree branch weapons
in case of werewolves, man
and I held your hand
while you made up your mind

through the burnt out shells of long ago parties
melted plastic and pentagram ruins
nothing is as depressing as a maze of pine
nothing feels as good as the first time

I don't remember anything specific
just the smell of fire
and the dreams that woke me up sweating
where you were dead.

Lights Underground

we made the lights low
everything got fuzzy and sidelong vivid
every time we threw a dart
it hit nowhere near a bullseye
but, we weren't really trying anyway
we were just kids
who'd survived the car crashes
laid-off veterans of telemarketing
mall rats and flea market drifters
tell me about your new tattoo
as if it was some kind of weird map
I'll quote dumb movies
from my VHS studies
C.H.U.D., Lethal Weapon 2
Deer Hunter, Goonies
we used to lay around
in the basements of your rotating parents
there'd be sounds above, some humans walking
down there the fish tank was always green
all the guitars were broken
and so were the drums skins
the power was out and by candle light
you made your life
worshipping the curled edges
of punk rock posters

we'd get high and stare at the curtains
that weren't really moving
search to find silverfish and 8-track cassettes
in water damaged boxes
sometimes when we talked it felt like a movie
other times, like an after school special
other other times, just two teenagers
under the influence of a pink moon
on a good night, we'd watch Conan O'Brien
knock back another six pack
feel the earth get frozen
while your cold dog barked out back
and we slowly fucked.

Curfew

"you can't get pregnant the first time"
we said it again, but didn't believe it
her curfew was over, I had my learner's permit
it was 10:05 PM, she was 3 weeks late
"drive me home, we'll tell her together"
12 newspapers frozen to my father's driveway
I had a 1988 Mercury Cougar
Thundercat symbol, bad heater coil
she shivered in her Power Puff Girl coat
I just drove, no radio, I just drove
as I turned to look at her acne'd face
the manic panic hair, steel braces
I didn't see something dying in the road
"oh!" she yelled, pointing
a wounded deer lifted its head
too late—crushed beneath the car
we kept driving, or I drove, she cried
at their house, she bolted
I muttered, "*no talk, I guess*"
back home, on the ice
and frozen newspapers
I started scraping the guts
from the undercarriage with a shovel
hair, red more red, steam, stench, antlers

I imagined this is what the doctors
would do to her in Cherry Hill
but at 2 AM, my phone rang
she said, "I just got it"
and I started to weep.

It Snows

Spout comes home
with a green suitcase
travel record player
we set it up in the pink room
next to the desk where I write
she dug around
came back with pinot noir
her eyes like little fires
I leaned back in the chair
saved from the garbage
cracked all my knuckles
except the broken one
the red chair wrapped her up
the radiator sang out
and I said, "we'll still be here
when the sun comes up,
take a seat"
"don't get comfortable"
she cooed, "though life is long"
"It's a trick" I said
"yup, it is"
I popped open the wine
with a Nike shoelace

a trick I learned on the internet
she pulled out her paints
one by one by one by one
then revealed a canvas
hidden behind the bookcase
"think I'll paint over this one"
"don't do that"
"then buy it from me"
"I'm broke"
"I'll take a million bucks"
she filled our coffee cups
with blood or crushed cherries
"or something," she said

I worked a rewrite over
hunting typos as she *sang*
let's spend the night together
neighbor knocking on the door
my foot stomping on the floor
"ignore the world, thursday nights
are for you and me"
"I know that," she said
pushing her long hair out of her eyes
as "Ruby Tuesday" came on
we noticed
that age old thing
all our teeth purple
paint all over the records
my fingers hurting from bad typing
no noise down in the street for once

and so we climbed out
onto the shaky fire escape
watched the snow falling
on 173rd street.

Not Leaving

10 PM in the snow
still driving, looking
searching for a spot
a girl walks out
keys in hand
"leaving?"
"no"

she walks up the block
tiny tracks in snow
I follow

"not leaving!" she yells

her keys jingle
the wind is not soft
she struggles uphill
I park

a kid comes out
an orange lit up stoop
snow lands in his hair
my headlights
look like a projector

by the frozen hydrant
he's leaning down now
the driver's side
of a blue Buick
I pull up
blinker on
he doesn't notice
what's taking so long?
"lock frozen?"
"wuh?"
I wanna say, "*pee on it*"
he finally says, "nah man,
not leaving"
he walks off
towards the chain-link
dog park
my wiper blades are shot
heater can't keep up
with my feet

I double park
hazards on
I go into my building
up the broken marble stairs
to our apartment
Spout is at the table
"still looking for a spot"
"put it in the garage!"
"fuck that"
"I'll give you the twenty bucks"

I kiss her, I go take a leak
when I come out
she hands me a cup of coffee
"couple more loops around"
I say, and take the trash
back down

climbing in my car
that's when I see
what the kid was writing
on the Buick
it says, FUCK YOU ROSA
YOUR A DUM BITCH
I don't wipe it off
who knows, it might be true

I make another loop.
Haven Ave to 168th street
left on Fort Washington
left on 177th, left on Haven
the mouth of the underground
garage glows gold
I can see the attendant, Shorty
shoveling off the ramp
he waves, I say, "Shorty, get some salt"
he says, "damn right, bro"
I cruise slow through the snow

no one leaves during a storm
no brake lights, or tail pipe smoke

only a man in a red coat
clearing snow to get ahead of tomorrow

but I see her coming back
she's still holding her keys
in the other hand a black plastic bag
"still not leaving!" she says
and then walks past me
to the blue Buick
and stares at the door
"what. the. fuck," she says
dropping the plastic bag

I don't laugh
there's a dull red glow
a block away
a foot on the brake
a tan Lexus leaving
I take the spot
on my way back
the blue Buick is wiped clean
temporarily.

Sidewalk

the super
shovels
the snow
covered
walk
revealing
our initials
carved into
once wet
concrete.

May 4th

we got married
in Jersey City
at a movie theatre
that was half-collapsed
and half-beautiful

she made
her own dress
and I wrote
my vows
on a parking ticket

as I buttoned my suit
I was sober
because the hotel bar
didn't open
till much later

friends blind folded me
and put me on a school bus
I sat in the back seat
holding Spout's hand
and we didn't talk

but she kissed me
despite what it did
to her lipstick

they took the blindfold off
when we got to the theatre
and she came down the stairs
and I looked up, and felt luckier
than a man surviving a 4,000 foot fall

I met her on movie house steps
you know
she was wearing a t-shirt
with a panther on it
and I had my hands in my pockets

during the ceremony
I promised to always save
her the last sip of coffee
unless she gave it to me as a gift

not a problem.

Yellow Table

I wanna wish us luck
I wanna wink a thousand times
and the wind outside to get wild
so the birds just lift
off the window ledge, float off
without flapping once

I wanna find coins in this pocket
and magic money in every jacket
I wanna awkwardly wave
making us strawberry blush
our cartoon eyes
cartoon wide

stay where you are
I'll come to you
the yellow table.

P.O. Box

all blue everything
a city peaking up
slow cabs and ambulances
a dog runs free
through the park
all white clouds
all across the sky
a woman screaming
at a sprinting
dalmatian
swinging its leash
above the grey mess
of her wild hair
as he
disappears
through the alley
all gold paint
in the foyer of my building
and a sign
hung
above my P.O. box
reading:
REWARD FOR LOST DOG
ANSWERS TO RUBY
DOES NOT FIGHT FIRES
$500.

I'm from Electric Peak, MT

sometimes you'll forget who you are
you'll go buy black rites candles
carving pentagrams on the linoleum floor
with a pulsing knife you found in the streets
as you put on Costa Rican coffee
and fill the sink with soap suds and hot water
the virgins you need will seem so far away

you'll start telling people you're from Montana
(instead of strip mall New Jersey)
Ekalaka, Ryegate, Swimming Women Road
say, "I'm from Electric Peak"
also feel free to try:
"Gunsight Mountain, every heard of it?"
Tell them you cut your teeth on a ranch
breaking wild horses, wait with baited breath
ask earnestly, "love me now?"

at the local college, sign up for a course
"Building Hot Air Balloons 101"
tell pretty girls at the bar, "baby, I'd like
to put your face on a hot air balloon
and release you up into the sky"
"that sounds nice," hopefully they'll say

or: go jump in pickup basketball games
on the asphalt court with the rusted net
behind the plaza with Fried Paradise
where you used to bread the chicken
after school for minim wage
and you knew exactly who you were.

31 Minutes

and just like that
I'm back from the dead
the power pills worked
the jumper cables
sent an explosion
up my crystalline spine
sudden goo leaked out
like cotton candy
your dog tried to eat it
but I am now a dog whisperer
and he or she listens
the hills are mine
I can order a pizza
and psychically make it arrive
1 minute past 30 minutes or less
free pizza pies
free pizza pies
you used to lay down beside me
now we hover electrically
in the space between Hell
and big country sky
where, each of my digits
is now a small nuclear bomb
that I'll use at the ATM

and when I text and drive
and when I don't floss
or flip a coin for good luck
status update:
I'm on the verge
of something good
and my spirit animal
is a typewriter
covered in my own blood.

An Illustrated Book of American Songbirds

I don't know what any
of these things are called
looking out the window
at the trees
I can pick out one
a pine tree
alright, so I know what a pine tree is
and I can look at all the birds
swooping around
sometimes if there's a blue one
I can say, "oh look, there's a bluejay"
I suppose I could spot a cardinal too
or a seagull
other than that...
the people
I don't know how to describe them
so I don't
the names of all the clever bones
in their faces
and the elaborate connections
to their distant homelands
I barely know about this town
and only know about this town

because the name's painted
in big block letters
on the water tower
these details
they're good to know
to reference, right?
I should get myself
an illustrated book
of American songbirds
I should get a comprehensive
field guide to the vegetation, too
low lying shrubs, weird grasses:
fancy vines with neon flowers
I'm supposed to have all
that stuff here, aren't I?
and the cars, I don't know
what any of the cars are
except the one I drive
I could tell you the make
and model of that one
all the others, I have no idea
so I should get a book on cars too
I should know all the *Kelly Blue Book* values
and projected mileage for each vehicle
it would help my writing dramatically
I'm going to get myself a current edition
of *The Chicago Manual of Style*
and I'm going to carefully study it
until I understand what a semicolon
could possibly be used for

I get the impression that would
really open new doors for me
and since my description of colors
is limited to the primary colors exclusively
with sometimes the word "neon"
stuck in there
I'm going to get myself a deluxe box
of 1,000 crayons and I'm gonna
spread them all out on the floor
and learn the names
of each of those colors
and I'm going to use them
to my advantage
yes
sickness, disease, suffering
I should interview a nurse
who works
the night shift at the ER
or I should just go to the ER tonight
for some reason
let me look around
to find a way to get myself hurt
I don't really want to get myself into a
motorcycle crash
but I feel like that kind of thing
would be good for my writing.

Other Birds

I

I'd like to catch a bird
accidentally
maybe while putting
a coat on, it fluttering in
(and staying)
—later—
even
flying around
the tower
of my shoulders
and me
distracted
finding
flowers falling
out of burnt up books
left on the radiator
outside on Haven
there's a light weeping up
from an icy sidewalk
across from the hospital
supposed
emergencies

meaning nothing
but the accidental bird
reads to me
as it flies
and as I walk
slipping good luck bits of rose
over my shoulder
into its sharp
strange beak
forever snapping

2

up there
I think
it flies
in loops
making
whatever
that infinity
symbol is
but I can't tell
as I study
nature
my phone
keeps
buzzing
on my lap

3

blue thread, green fuzz
shoelace, shiny metal
bits of glass, mouse fur
the things you build
to keep yourself
warm in the fucking rain
and through the weird night
also: pieces of lint
from some heaven
unknown
as the doomed say
"*whatever works.*"

Takeout

the bomb shelter
beneath our building
is filling up
with takeout menus
from new restaurants
that won't survive
the end of the world.

Spring

we go walking in the rain
sharing an umbrella
with New Jersey on it
it becomes a long walk
everything
unexpectedly green
again.

Talking to People You'll Never See Again at Parties

I said, "she's a neurosurgeon
and I'm an oral surgeon"
another time, I said
"I just got laid off from Megadeth"
mostly, I say, "I'm a garbageman"
no one wants to talk about that
and that's what I like
we can talk
about anything
else then.

A Cool Fictional Character

for a while
be a cool fictional character
don't worry or over-study
grocery store oranges
for their green spots
or flat spots or whatever
just walk, hands in your pockets
whistling the theme
to *The Andy Griffith Show*
The Fishin' Hole, it's called
three suggestions:
get real kind
pet every dog
pick every unwatched rose
carrying it in your teeth
on your march up
137th street.

Summer

when the hydrants open
I'll take you out of the city
I've found our car
and thrown your suitcase
off the fire escape
together we'll cross the bridge
bright lights and mixtapes
the turnpike vaporizing
a motel awaiting
somewhere
just gotta find it
the ocean is darkest
just before the dawn
then, I'm drunk and hanging out
on the balcony
while you put on your neon bikini
and the neon light
in the parking lot flickers
summers in New Jersey
I get my deepest wishes
fulfilled at random vending machines
the greatest joy I feel
the desk girl
knocking at the door

"can you keep it quiet
we're getting complaints"
and we keep going
louder than ever.

Swimmers

spiked watermelon juice
the world again, wet with dew
at this time
the girls come swimming after you
tell them anything
put your mouth to their hearts
hum strange secret hymns.

Purple Gel Tab

rocking out in a parked car
to the broken radio
bubbling out harsh static only

I have a crumbled up note
in one of these pockets
that says:
"TOMORROW I GAIN YOUR RESPECT
AFTER IT RAINS
WE'LL MEASURE THE LAWN
THE CLOUDS WILL SMILE PROUD
WHEN YOU COLLAPSE
FALL IN MY STUPID DIRECTION"

toxicology report:
still high on things
that were cool 15 years ago
but perfectly fine
with it right now

items I'm looking for in the glovebox:
bleach that works on our lives
road maps back
nostalgic sparks
flying out of the bed springs

call-in requests:
if I say, you're the chosen one
do something shiny
my punk rock years were spent
kicking crud on supposed
civil war battle fields
flanked by pine trees

Spout knocks on the window
"come on in, girl"
it's a miracle that these doors
still open, but they do
she sits and joins me

with a flick of the wrist
she turns the dial
and there is music.

Sonny and Cher Sing "I Got You Babe"

the trouble goes away
walking up the hill
in the sideways rain
the thought of Spout
coming north
while I go south
intersect at our dim bar
beer and jukebox music
meet at the door
days sucked into bottomless pits
nights blooming up, glowing
our worry exploding
into red smoke
and heavy fire
as we thin our blood
and float up over the saw blades
rotating around us, uselessly.

Low Light

what you want and what you get
are different under different lights
we hang around the skeleton of the jukebox
thankful this is a dark bar
because in natural light, you are ugly
and I am too, crooked spines
knuckles busted, lips split
but our lies are beautiful enough
for us to be in true love
in the low light.

Music

got drunk on your birthday
got full of weird light on Tuesday
and again on All Saint's Day
whenever that is
god is in a bad band
that gets booked
wherever we're drinking
his angels drown us out
bathed on stage in hot pink light
this smoke machine spells your name
up towards all the gooey stars
excuses:
got behind on the rent
got a worse car
that no one would steal
got a battery for the fire alarm
got more coffee, got more cream
all the words I know
to all the best songs
are the wrong lyrics
when you reveal the right ones
I no longer like the song
update:
sobered up on my birthday.

Nilsson

if your blood becomes red wine
slide into the room in white socks
with nothing else on
drop the needle on Harry Nilsson
Nilsson Schmilsson, 1971
shake around wild
until something pops
never mind it's 3 AM Wed. night
keep saying, "if I die, let it be
during 'The Moonbeam Song.'"

Other People's Mail

opening other people's mail
for entertainment, reading letters
addressed to neighbors
small, shallow things, those letters
bad handwriting, details of
insignificant things
better than watching daytime TV
or walking up the hill for beer
and we only get one channel anymore
the rest are snow static
the mailman is a lost man
he makes mistakes on our accounts
sometimes I pass the heavy woman
in 11B, she won't look me in the eyes
she's the one who's been intercepting
my subpoenas and ransom notes
that's okay, I get all her birthday cards
and once, a postcard from France
sent from someone named Oliver
last year, for Christmas, she got
bad gift certificates, that I still
haven't used
out on the stoop
is the kid who plays the drums

he's waiting for a ride
or the ice cream man, or weed
all of the above
I'd offer him a ride
but I haven't been able to find my car
for quite awhile
I got a notice from his school
he's failing pre-calculus
that's fine
he probably gets my love letters
sent from my wife
and flushes them down the toilet
we know more about the others
in the building
than we know
about ourselves.

Not in Service

no riders. no jokes. lights out
no run around Sally. no rose tattoos
no bluebirds. a lack of respect for sleep

no concern for on time delivery
no feel good golden emergencies, only mice
only bugs looking around in beer bottles
mistaking cigarette butts for snack

no air conditioning, no office romance
no getting shot out of cannons
into your welcoming arms
no hi-fi stereo equipment. no soap
no way to convince an unconcerned party

no long lost love returning from the grave
no safety nets. no jet fuel. no ice
no up to the second system analysis
no underground tunnel to the corner store
I'll have to take the sidewalk

no goodbye kiss. no bulletproof vest
no warm tuna milk for the cat we don't own
no secret handshake or birthday cake
all I have is this crippling love for you.

Wife

it's easy to believe in you
you're all I can understand
most days
you're not a car salesman
you're not a police officer
you're not the super
you have no faith
in the great beyond.

Extra Ladder

we learn in the fires
it hurts but has to happen
we have to sleep lightly
smoke in the hallways
circuits crossed
exposed wiring
glasses of water everywhere
well, beneath the bed
I keep an extra ladder
and on the wall
I have, a calendar full of starred days
of tall chances to misplace my wallet
somewhere non-sacred
out there in the briars
if you help me look
I'll help you look
plenty of time after work
the police tow our cars
to some secret place
that's fine, the train runs all night
and I can see the river
from my window
if I lean out, all is silver

your kiss, your time, your patience
we inspect our fire extinguishers
every fucking night.

Making Out

slowly building something
some days I feel like it's a tiger tank
other times a wooden model of a stegosaurus
pushing sand around, making anthills
making piles of obsidian rock
dividing seashells
as all the streetlights flicker off
electric tools in an uninsulated room
the sound carries everywhere
ricocheting off the neighbors
the basketball courts
floating
clutched in the beaks of dizzy birds
wobbling after the moon
I don't have blueprints
and there's not really anyone to ask
you can point in any direction
spin around, eyes obscured
surgical mask
these pieces make something,
sometimes it looks like a monster truck
mostly I think
it's a box of lightning

with the lid sealed shut
I leave it for you
at the foot of your bed
every chance I get.

Effective

let us be effective
at rolling dice
at stealing glances
at lifting cups
to find hidden coins
let us be graceful
on the parallel bars
seldom falling
but if we do
into the bows
of tug boats
floating
on our silver river
slipping
underneath
the white light bridge
it's true, we're dumb as rocks
but somewhere
cheerleaders
cheer for us
and if we know no better
than to let the wrong one in
we'll welcome

anyone
into our nest
amid the ruins
of supposed Heaven.

Taxi

I

I hailed a cab at 4:30 AM
falling out of a bar
on a cobblestone side street
"need to go uptown, way far uptown"
the driver said, "I'm new"
I said, "just drive forever,
I'll tell you when"
"okay"
"point this car, second star to the right
and straight on till morning"
"oh"
"173rd street and Haven Ave"
"got it"
the GPS went beep beep beep
in the backseat my eyes shuttered
and the radio and dashboard
and streetlights slipping past
all had a different glow
going away

2

"wake up!" the cabbie said
"wuh, wuh?" I sat up
everything spun
until everything came into slow focus
out the window: suburban houses
and the sun
"we're lost"
"lost? where are we?"
"lost"
I looked up at the GPS, all black
"use your phone"
"no phone," he said
a sign read, Sycamore Street
"we're at Sycamore Street," he said
"what town?" I asked
he held his hands up in defeat
"go back, we'll figure it out"
"we're in a neighborhood, I can't
figure out what way out of the maze"
"fuck it, drive around
let's look for a landmark"

all the houses were the same
small variations in shade
"you should have woken me"
"my pride, my foolish pride"
there were no dog walkers
there were no joggers

it was 6 AM, it started raining
"pull over here, I'll knock
…wait, though, man—wait"
"of course, I need you to get back"
"Jesus"
I walked down the driveway
and knocked on a red door
a man in a bathrobe answered
"can I help you?"
"see that cab?"
"sure."
"I got in that cab on Great Jones Street
and Bowery, New York City"
"okay…"
"where the fuck are we?"
"Mt. Kisco"
"we're lost"
he laughed, "hold on"
when he came back
he had directions written on the back
of a pancake house receipt

I climbed up front
in the passenger seat
"here's how we go, it's easy"
I flapped the directions in the air
like magical currency
"thank fucking god"
"and on the way home…" I said, "we'll stop"
he nodded "gas and breakfast"

3

at Pancake Palace,
I got the corned beef
hash and eggs
the driver, whose name was Paul
got the garden omelet with bacon
we split the blueberry pancakes
they brought us out like, thirty
the coffee was alright
just alright
sugar was needed.

You Do Great Good

you do great good
you flip the record over
rescue the needle from the hissing
popping netherworld
place it in the groove again

you keep me close
like a balloon without a string
used as a bible to stop a bullet
held, protecting your heart
clamped between
your thin-wristed arms
covered in near invisible fuzz

I will have clouds for eyes
I am out of service, just awaiting grace
there is an electric hum
passing through me
but I've crash landed through Heaven
through the weird sky
through brick walls
and I'll lay here aching
until you lay down too
then everything is fine.

Too Much

retirement plan:
don't ever die
drink this juice
from this wolf paw footprint
let's fucking party

tarot card reading:
any minute now
there will be a tidal wave of euphoria
and you won't have to worry
until you run out of beer again

system analysis:
get up, do jumping jacks
talk fitness, give out free advice
about skipping stones
paint over rust, practice bird calls
lie, sleep, keep being interesting
as if they won't try
to assassinate you for it

the next morning:
I'll be late for work

but I'll do it in style
descending from a ladder
swinging out of a helicopter
this is all just
a very strange side effect
from a very good drug

night life:
be known for
folding up love-letters
releasing them
out into the jet stream
like actual jets
aimed at sleeping skylines.

To Succeed

to somehow
succeed
you have
to keep
jumping up
and down
in a crowded room
until everybody else
gets tired of jumping
and you're the only one
still jumping
try it, sometime
the secret
is to wear
spring shoes.

These Things Take Time

things work out, they have to
days get blue, a gravel hill
taking the dog for a walk
though you don't have a dog
find people who talk
pass bottles, pass codes
pass all the small hope
open it up, find rows
and rows of want
rewind tapes, consult charts
confessions from the bottomless pits
of the human heart
send signals with smoke
the ground-up dust
from a feral rose
breathe in perfect sync
only step where I step
failed and flailed
but think we're on the cusp
if we release a thousand birds
that don't fly up
let's try another coat of paint
another year in the road
getting used to getting bruised

till everything feels good
these things take time
I wrote, you wrote
we rolled all the heavy stones
end over endless end
up towards the waiting cloud line.

All the Perfect Music

right on time, you arrive
a second later—the world would've ended
but now, things are good

such as: beer on ice, low lights
your tan skin accented by aquamarine lace
oh—and golden oldies
rolling through the warm tubes
and you, doing all the corresponding moves
to all the perfect music

that's life
when you're living like
all your blood's been drained
and replaced with red wine
and everything's the opposite of riot

'cause the windows are open
and somehow there's a breeze
that carries in the smell of the ocean
but we're nowhere near the ocean

so—slow dance horizontal
on the golden velvet couch

we're never taking
the christmas lights down
I'm not just a square peg
you're not just a round hole
the song ends, another comes on
this one's my favorite
cross my heart and hope you squirt
master the art of calling out of work
teach me the gospel of rock and roll
while my mind is clear and open
and awaiting further instructions.

Exact Sciences

we come up from the mud
towards the surface in the rain
you and me and our unadjusted eyes
our patience, our inside jokes
our access denied
there's a subtle difference
between right and wrong
often bathed in smoke
big things
we don't talk about
because we'd rather just have fun
calm down
yes, there's a fire in the apartment
but it's in the other room
we have time
lay back down.

Antitoxin

your laugh
in the other room
on the telephone
walls can't absorb it all
floors echo it to me
the ceiling is filling
inflating
it's life
I'll probably live
100,000 years
because of
your laugh.

Third Rail Alive

the subway
may never come
I'll spend
my after-life
on an empty
platform
leaning on
a broken-tiled column
hands forever
tucked in pockets
me: third rail alive
you: way up in the sky
on the 456th floor
at your desk, I bet
wondering
where I am
well, all I can say
I'm on my way.

Your Changes Have Been Saved

prayer book:
don't worry anymore
practice not looking towards the door
in between major disasters
I'll find you, in the calm
of the gold foyer
and wait for you
on the radiator

blind date:
you'll recognize me right away
I'll be the guy with the bubblegum in his hair
the suit of armor full of bullet holes
the advice that doesn't line up

let's leave this party:
are you available only in certain moonlight?
can we talk anyplace else besides the bathtub?
what gemstones are you built from?
what keys work where?
and for what?
cops seem to circle this building
tell me about the secret tunnels beneath
we might have to use them

evening news:
occasionally get lost
in high pursuit of yourself
the trick is to take it easy
and then run the red lights
losing the police
brakes screeching in the rain
at least that's how
they do it in the movies

our green bedroom:
from time to time, get so pleased
magic slick sheets, no fire
something materializing
well-meaning and strange
Spout leaning over, saying
your changes have been saved.

Opera

comes through
the green wall
a neighbor
doing
voice scales
in his
mirrored
hall

when we first
saw this
apartment
one tenant
told us
"he's a *tenore spinto*"
"oh" I said
"and he only sings
in the nude
at home anyway"
"how do you know?"
"brought his mail over once"

it's been nine years
I still shred all his mail.

Keys

at first
we had to learn
how the locks
worked
feels
like a lifetime ago
now
it's all automatic
something
the wrist
just knows
in an envelope
I'll send you spares
that won't work
for you, for years.

Between Liftoffs

not a good talker
not a good listener
but I've been known to read
anything laying around
the backs of cereal boxes
instruction manuals
to steam carpet cleaners
warnings
material safety data sheets
booklets accompanying
old school
Nintendo cartridges

I don't paint straight
and I can't sort things alphabetically
numerically or accurately
but I'm alright at ping pong
and I'm pretty good
at standing there
watching cars try to park
parallel on the street
while I sip a beer
from some kind
of magical aluminum can

it's just day after day
watching dusty ideas
sailing down the silver river
placing cracked records
on the turntable
so they wobble and rotate
around the room
I make no plans
come into focus

I scan bus schedules
though I have a car
I leaf through old magazines
left down on the radiator
looking for articles, advertisements
anything, even the table of contents
just something to keep me interested
until there's something
glowing deathly neon
to write about.

Ordinary War

no idea
just waiting in a parked car
not at a stop light
not anywhere
near a green one either
no idea
done joking around
done talking nonsense
done being serious too
life is a series
of infinite possibilities
reduced to a few
wonderful compromises
you be cool
I'll be cool
if we die in a combat zone
was there anything
that really needed to be written
that close to a land mine?

Stereo Up

days arrive like small puzzles
each chess piece has black wings
that sprout when the moon comes out
just fly away: too soon
but I'll remember your kiss
how you gave me your last dollar
I took off your left shoe
you slipped off your right
on the front stoop we shared an apple
then moved to the golden velvet couch
arm in arm, like prison guards
in love with an empty jailhouse
"doomsday's just a myth"
feeling good despite the worst
whispering low with the stereo
sayin', sayin', sayin'
"drink this, drink this, drink this"
when times get rough
I think of you naked
each part of your body, a clue to solve
some big thing, floating in the ether
kill rust. break bricks
eat dust. spit foam. sip lava
drink this.

I Like Your Shoes

life lesson:
try not
to get stared
at too hard

blue print:
random loose fittings, collapsible
buildings—step over the debris
put the sun in your hair like a flower

after school special:
be on all the posters on all the walls
of all the teens, draw your silhouette
across the lids of all the sleeping cities

record sleeve:
we rode the short bus together, shared
rashes, shared rations—fell in and out
of love, misinterpreted the same lyrics

tech support:
grew apart, grew lichen, grew closer
gold teeth, go in peace, everything
ripe and raw with dew for you

transit map:
now spin the entire Earth on a single
outstretched finger—be my favorite
Harlem Globetrotter

take out menu:
start out small
spread out into the air
cover it all, a well meaning wildfire.

Reaction

there are times when I hear music
and nothing dances but my own hope
the people are so very quiet
only in love with their own shoes
but nothing else
I can't help but steal their mail
and I can't help but leave their window open
so when they finally let their birds out
the birds find the world
instead of just the house.

Don't Worry

I am warned of insects
disturbing wasps and hornets
waking up fire ants
and people too, at certain moments
can be worse than water moccasins
or king cobras

they say
there are bottomless pits on earth
containing all the loss
anyone can handle
I am passed a note in the subway
detailing this
on graph paper:
"EVERY YEAR IT GETS WORSE
ARE YOU PLANNING FOR IT?
IF YOU'RE NOT PLANNING FOR IT
YOU'LL BE THE FIRST TO GO"
sometimes it's as if
we live in a hand-made maze
but know certain walls
would never move

so we keep a bomb or two
in our back pocket
or in her fluorescent purse
to make your own route
when the rules fail us
dead ends open up to happy hour

there are small moments
when it feels like the killer bees
are finally here
and there's no good
that'll come crawling up
from the rocks beneath the rushes
of the evening rumors
I don't worry
oh, I don't
when you get close
people aren't any closer
to a wild animal
than you are
and I don't worry
if things collapse
I get the impression
that there's water running
under everything
and that we could use
our bodies
together
as a raft.

Not an Accident

real love is a car crash
that you survive
whether the air bags deploy
or you go through the windshield
or explode on impact

I feel everything stop
and I go out on the pavement
to watch the emergency crews
cut the roof of the car off
with a K-10 saw
they peel back the sheet metal
as if it was a can of tuna fish
and they were in the mood
for a sandwich

when they look inside
and see us all torn apart
and crushed
will it be odd
for them to note
we're still holding hands?

Spout

I always wanted a gun
now I got you
and you're a beauty
I aim you at animals
then drag them
into the fire
you set
inside the cage
of my ribs.

By a Fire

your cheerleader prayers
and your communion song book
adorned with medals of war
devoid of bluebirds
I'm a dog of mud puddles
a cry slips through my teeth
that no museum preserves
that no cop shines his shine light
that no devil opens like a can of tuna
to suck the fish water
into a mouth wide cursed
your kiss of gold
sets my skull into decision
in this place I'm settled
in this place I'm yours
shake your pom-poms on me
sing your song of god way out of key
pet my wet fur and scratch the fear
from behind my supersonic ears
I am a transporter of insects
and a sideline watcher
your gift of fire.

Defense Mechanism

when things hurt
it's easier to be funny
than to sit there dying
with everybody looking
all the glory of medicine
and the threat of rain
the mice in the walls and
parking fines unpaid
why does everybody have a balcony
to watch us, waiting for them to leave?
why don't we put up some iron ore curtains
to keep out the neighborhood radiation?
I get the feeling that if the fire
is not in your apartment
it's going to be everywhere else
so lets just stay in
rather than turn to ash
when things hurt
it's easier to be funny
than to sit there dying
with everybody looking.

Best Kind of Curse

I will be your only friend
if everybody else puts their hearts
back in their suitcases
I'll still be on the street
with a space for you in my arms
and a notch for you in my spine
I don't blame you at all
though it'd be easy to accuse you
of rain clouds and extinctions
you're a comfort to me
when everybody else is a scab
that I can't help picking till it's a scar
you know a lot about my dog
and I fed your cat while you were away
even though I wanted him to die
love is a battery jumped by another car
that finds you on the side of the road
love is the frozen meat
thawing on the counter
love is the search for missing persons
after major disasters
though common sense says they're dead
no common sense in love

I'll take/save the change out my pockets
to buy you a bulletproof vest
for judgement day stitched with roses
I'll paint the hospital bed your favorite color
then I'll burn it
so you never have to lay in it again
I'll catch all of the birds
and make them into a blackbird pie
but you won't have to eat it
if you don't like, just know why

you're a saint in my nights
when everybody else
has devoured my birthday cake

love is the guesstimates that are
somehow 100% accurate
and allow the sun through the fog
to come back up

love is a broken window
that we climb through
to get out of the goddamn rain
love is getting stabbed in the neck
and having somebody
to seal the wound with their mouth
so you can never die.

Listening

the apartment windows open
below, people talking on the stoop
they live inside their low voices
but we can hear everything

circular discussions
about baseball, astral projection
something falling off the moon

we can't see the moon from in here
and tonight the fire escape
isn't safe to stand on
so we use our imaginations

it's that kind of night
you can practically hear a person whistling
for their dog to come in from the backyard
across the river in New Jersey

the cars drive by needing brake jobs
uncut rotors squeeeeeeeeeell
street animals climb
down the storm drain
panting, tails whipping

aluminum garbage can lids
ricochet downhill
doing good, escaping
to the river
and then the sea beyond

if we're quiet and we listen
we'll notice the buzzer go off
when someone enters our building
"is it the 1-7-3 Killer?"
"is it the pizza-man?"
"pizza-person," I correct

someone outside unlocks a parked car
it goes "chirp, chirp"
and even though
I have a spot already by the dog park
I smile as a parking spot
right outside the building opens

I lean out the window
and say, "will one of you guys stand
in that spot while I move my car?"

they move from the stoop to the spot
continuing their conversation there
Spout tosses the car keys to me
from the nest at the yellow table
there is calypso and opera out in the hall.

Dominoes

give me something
brittle little empty envelopes
coins flattened on railroad tracks
keys to forgotten cities
underneath the earth
I'll show you pilot lights
that we can relight
I'll bring you up to the roof
point out birds on fire
gliding through the night
in turn, give me clues
tracing paper traced with lemon juice
a map of the highway of your neck
leading down the front of your shirt
to somewhere with fog
in the mornings, every morning
every morning, give me time
I'm slow like vines growing down a hill
looking for the bottom
so I can scale a rusted fence
over the power lines
up towards the hint of the moon
I'll leave out directions for you
so you can circle the neighborhood

left turn after left turn
after left turn after left turn
until you are right back here
where there is coffee
for the both of us.

Thanks for Making Me Feel Like Cool Hand Luke Today

for a while, I feel useless
in the slowed down time
between liftoffs
so I occupy myself with records
while chipping the wall out
with baby rattle rock-hammers
hidden in the middle
of the super's bible
alright, enough of it
I blink and snap out of it
see, I got a real old
landline telephone
it's broke, and dark red
just like your lipstick
you don't ever wear that lipstick
very often
but you do leave me
the most pleasant love letters
smeared in curly cues
all across our bathroom mirror
when I wake up
I always find you gone
but I can always find out

what you're thinking
just by your handwriting
all across the walls
down the halls, leading out
into the always, unexpected
brightness of today

once in awhile
I go out to the car
and find you've painted it
a new color
it'll be green instead of orange
and then teal instead of cream
it's then that you've got me
when you've really got me
and I'd do just about anything
except die

I always feel like
Cool Hand Luke
when I try my key
in this strange ignition
and it works

at what intersection
am I meeting you?

Sing to Me

the rain comes down
we stay out of it while we can
but sometimes we have to go out
to wash the soot from our mouths

the days are quiet
as we re-wire the stereo
sing me a song while I splice wires
I'll tap along with my free hand
we sure can make speakers explode
isn't it true?

life is slow

just because it's something
we don't understand
try not to call it a miracle

the wind threatens to break our window
I'm not worried,
I've got you to be my human shield
If we get flooded out
Just climb on my back
I can swim for at least a block

just when you expect nothing
other than an execution
new buds come out of brick walls
glowing unexpected green.

For My Friend Who's Still Alive

everybody thinks about death
considering, contemplating
weighing it on little scales
we keep in our pockets
daily, in the sunlight
when the streetlights come on, too
there can be comfort in knowing
nothing lasts forever
it casts these days here
in-between, in gold
and over the molten lava
we often hover
our desires never sealed in amber
till we say so

I'm glad you didn't jump.

No Plans

I don't make plans
if i do, I won't make it
out of the city
out of the maze of the Heights
I draw no maps
I own no mirror
better drape a robe
around the circumference
of the soot wind curse
better carry a mystery flask
in your florescent purse
I don't trust people
who don't poison
themselves slowly
with escape snake smoke
I'm an ace shot
with the skeleton gun
and settle
for no sugar substitute
because the cancer rats
need no company
build up tolerance, by day
leave the bomb shelter, by night
search the sidewalk

for the panels
where we left our initials
long ago, once wet
cement.

True Believer

I am the true believer
I am the true believer
give me a tuna fish sandwich
a paper carton of Yoo-hoo
and the keys to our lost car
I am the true believer
with hands custom molded
to fit on your golden breasts
on ripe golden apples
and down your polyester pants
I am the true believer
I am the true believer
loan me a fin and a lighter
a deck of tarot cards
with goat-headed naked girls
a bottle not to drink
just to break against
the entrance to the bomb shelter

legend has it
I am the true believer
I've got a leaky faucet and I don't care
I've got bubble gum to put in your hair
the dead are dead for a reason

we are alive, wet and ripe
magic fruit always in season
you are without doubt
I am the true believer

this street used to lead somewhere
now the corner store is closed
and our dreams are pulled
down the silver river
in dark tug boats
at least the bombs
land somewhere else
I am here to take out the trash
we'll spell off with the dishes
when the record ends
put on another
for the true believer.

A Week

*SATURDAY

a day in bed, play sick/be sick
pizza for breakfast, Robitussin lunch
call up the liquor store on the phone
"two bottles of pinot noir
I got twenty-five dollars
however far that gets me"
"it'll get you to California
but not to France"
pajamas, faux fur lined moccasins
coffee pot after coffee pot
I wanna be killed by the city
early, for my birthday

desperate messages
from Russian brides
blinking in the sidebars
seeking love in America
is this a test from god?

Pauley Shore on VHS
Joy Division cassettes, Mulder
Dominican chickens, Scully
Reese's Peanut Butter Cups

Nightmare on Elm Street poster
puffer fish, dogs still lost in the trees
light the doomsday ghostly lanterns
it's colder outside than it looks
a hooded sweatshirt is a suit of armor
Let it Ride with Richard Dreyfuss
Our Rolling Stones vinyl *Hot Rocks*
has a jagged chip cracked off
so be diligent: when you get to "Wild Horses"
shit's about to get real ½ way through
the chorus
extra blanket heat not on yet
the super comes up at 7, says
"the guy in the next apartment died
so if you knew him, he's dead now"
I say, "I don't know anybody in real life
just on the computer"

*SUNDAY

devour paperback universes
watch my girl tongue-tie
the stems of cherries
no football or baseball
or political discussions
just bedroom laying
coffee cup poison
John Hughes advice
Steak-umms on english muffins

order gem stone field guides
Audubon bird books
¾ length pony baseball T's
don't shave, don't complain, don't worry
just flip the record, and keep loving me
we broke the washing machine
we crashed the car
we lost the spare keys
we dropped the ball
and have no idea how
we're gonna hide our mutations
and it's almost Halloween
we're misplaced

we're outta sorts
somebody lend me some latex
if I get you pregnant
let's name the baby Ace

make some popcorn
put on T-Rex
start a fire though
we don't have a fireplace
digging in boxes for loose leaf paper
photographs of you
when you were young
you're still young
throw some popcorn
up into the air
I'll grab it like a wolf
catching a rabbit peaking out a hole

talk awhile about life after death
infomercials, telemarketing
negotiations: they'll ever die
only in the movies
make a phone call to Texas
talk to my brother
so glad when he answers
and says he'll come to visit

*MONDAY

I put on my army coat
I dust off my neon sneakers
got the garbage in one hand
a cartoon shark mug in the other
coffee, black coffee, 4 AM
as I come down the marble stairs
door slams
in the foyer of my building
are junk magazines
books on C++ programming,
tour pamphlets for New Mexico
guy somewhere somehow (someone)
died somewhere in the building
there's a little note:
"TAKE WHAT YOU WANT, THIS BELONGED TO
THE DEAD GUY, THE REST WILL GO TO CHARITY"
I look but I find nothing, I walk out
into the rain

umbrella shaped like new jersey
rain overflowing the drain
same old city, where'd I leave my car?
what street? 173? 174?

Demi Moore used to look good
long ago
glossy *People* magazine on the radiator
that's what you get in our building
when you die
I wonder "is he the one who always ordered
Indian food?
oh, yes, my car: corner of 172
I should have remembered 172
what is C++? would it help me? should I go
back and get it?
I'm going to New Mexico
should have taken that tour guide book?
something leaves little clues for you
but they just lead to more clues
and more clues and more clues
and more clues and
Surrrrrrrrrrrrrrrrrrrender to
the morning commute
rolling through the neighborhood
approaching the White Light Bridge
windshield wipers malfunctioning
Rolling Stones on the stereo
"I forgot my lunch" look in the back seat
"fuck" look on the floor, "fuck
I'll have to eat off the roach coach truck"

Mick Jagger says: "bring me dead flowers
to my wedding…and I won't forget
to put roses on your grave"

Jersey turnpike, rolling towards the oil refinery
weave in and out of traffic, steering with my
knee, thinking:
"was he the guy whose mail I used to get?
the nameless faceless one, behind the door to
apartment 14B?"

*TUESDAY

duck out of work early
make it out the gates of
the oil refinery
gravel lot
chain link fence
mimic Steve McQueen
in *The Great Escape*
fires from the flare stack
burning up the white sky
got my car keys in one hand
checking my phone with the other

my girl is on a train
from the city
coming to me
Linden, New Jersey

try to time it right
be there, waiting at the station
take her west
for a car ride
wedding business
but first, we'll navigate
through a maze of blocks
red lights, stop signs, gang kids
lounging on stoops
trash cans, basketballs hoops
what a strange place to have to live
industrial row house
chipped brick wall waste
cross over 1 & 9
cut through the 99 cent store lot
Wood Ave, gas 'n' go, office stationary
post office, Army/Navy
a park with no lakes and no swans
I park under an unidentifiable
shade tree
my neon sneakers kicked out in front
sitting on the last of the green grass
drinking a Dunkin' Donuts coffee
I smell like fuel
but I can't tell
cars running/windows down
stereo growls
Bruce Springsteen insinuating
"This is my hometown…
this is my hometown"
keep checking my silver Timex Indiglo

everything in life is supposedly scheduled
not much longer now
her time, her light, her life, her mouth
looking up the rails for Spout
when the train comes in
she's the last one on the platform
flower dress
dark hair, dark everything
sea green Day-Glo purse
she takes my hand, says
"want me to drive?"
"no," I say, "I need you to navigate
and play music"
Spout nods, "that's much more
important, you're right"
any direction will work
but we can only get there
set to the perfect soundtrack

*WEDNESDAY

Wednesday
on payday
all our problems
temporarily lift
and everything
becomes a ladder
that leads
wherever we wish

*THURSDAY

clicking around the internet aimlessly
free association, Queen under pressure
David Bowie
trying to figure out
what to be for Halloween
which demon, which ghost
where we going? where we rolling?
big suit, David Bryne, record reviews
lusting for my time machine
a meet up with 1976 Deborah Harry
drinking pumpkin beer
like a pumpkin patch pimp
hanging with Spout in the pink room
new chair from "the dead guy"
that was out at the curb
"think there's bed bugs in it"
"it's a chair"
"bed bugs can still be in a chair"
"oh, chair bugs?"
"totally has chair bugs"
Astral Weeks, Moondance
Van Morrison sings like a saxophone
guy couldn't have been human
"everyone everyone everyone everyone
everyone everyone everyone everyone"
Royal Tenenbaums
"Ethel, baby—I *am* dying"
Gene Hackman says to Anjelica Huston

Spout gets up and goes to make burritos
she puts on Daft Punk and I hear
the chopping, the sizzling
the "Harder Better Faster Stronger"
I'm rolling around on my trash found
dead-guy chair, thinking about lit mags
to submit to
sometimes I feel lost
website after website
popping new beers
at the table she says, "I'm gonna be neon
Medusa"
"badass"
"what'll you be?"
"*Evil Dead 2*"
I'm dumb and numb and happy
we dance around the living room
until the white lady
downstairs
comes up to complain
then, we move to the gold couch
just talking, talking, talking
when I fall asleep
I dream of today
and can feel her kiss my eyelids

* FRIDAY

hang out in the rain
not worried about anything
books I should be reading
things I should be finishing
too many projects
too much hope on the line
there a buzz in all the blood
if you keep your heart open
there's a truth to learn
don't care to look stupid
all the ways you are here for me
all the ways I misplace the car keys
life is just a typo
that everyone edits a different way
be careless and be unoriginal
and don't walk too straight
take every chance to stumble
laugh at all you come across
forget all the bad times
glow neon un-doomed and
shake yourself 'til something pops.

Off-Key

enjoy it till it's gone
get out what we can
beauty piled up
on the side of our street
pigeons becoming
relentless in the eaves
mice venturing out
of the walls
different graves
dug for you and me
but we kick the dirt back in
when no one is looking
hands linked, off-key singing
danger tape, caution tape
supposed death under construction
every night eating birthday cake
blowing out our candles
enjoying each other
in the darkness
and more so
in the light.

Love Song of the Insane

I sat for hours
leaning against
the Chinese food
restaurant brick wall
next to a pay phone
that hadn't worked
since before I was born

killing time on 181st street
close enough to the river
to hear the tug boats
and the cars on the bridge
but in an awkward place
between the tenement rows
where I couldn't see the water
strange how I'm always
waiting for you

when you come around
and shoot me out of your cannon
my body will sing the love song of the insane
as it strikes this graffitied brick wall
my blood will gather in pools
for the grey pigeons to avoid

when the cop comes back up the sidewalk
and wants to know what I'm still doing here
I'll say, "I'm killing time in America
and singing the love song of the insane
waiting for a call to come in
on this pay phone that hadn't worked
since before I was born"

despite the threat of rain
.probably all night I'll be
alternate side and third rail alive
with the orange lights appearing
in boxed windows
and the shadows of women
standing up in their kitchens
and the passenger side window
smashed out of this parked blue Buick
all day I've been filling myself
with brave poison
waiting for you to come around
and help me figure out
how the chorus goes
to the love song of the insane
you can sing it alone all you want
but it just doesn't sound right

on Haven Avenue they're selling
unripened fruit
immortally not in season

I'll eat another, tastes like
how your heart does

when the sun goes all the way down
the kid who owns the Buick
comes up the sidewalk
"SOMEBODY SMASHED IN MY
WINDOW!"
he is right, he is so dead on right
somebody did in fact smash in his window
his passenger side window to be exact
"LOOK AT THIS SHIT!"
I tell him that I've been waiting all day
"WAITING? WAITING FOR WHAT!"
"oh nothing, just killing time in America
and waiting to see your reaction"

I tell him I've been waiting for my baby
to shoot me out of a cannon
into this brick wall
I explain that I've been thinking
about all the small animals
on the bottom of the ocean
filling themselves with brave poison
prepared to go on up to the surface
he doesn't understand a word
of what I'm saying
he's used to hearing simple
top 40 hit songs

he's not accustomed
to the love song of the insane

shame, oh shame
I'm happy when he drives away
leaving a pile of glass diamonds
and nothing else

I eat an eggroll as the moon
comes over, scraping the top
of a tilted building
I'm trying to decrypt the language
behind your teeth
of shadow and lazy graffiti
I'm thinking about your neck
and your laugh that fills our rooms
pink: green: orange
falling like this
art: sleep: living

I'm thinking about how
you would look
coming up the sidewalk
and then you do

you say, "I was calling you all day"
"on that phone right there?"
"yeah, that one exactly"
"I didn't hear it ring I've been busy
singing the love song of the insane"

she's got a job, I don't have a job
I kill my time here without grace
filled with poison, sitting near
the silver river
she leans against the wall with me
and asks, "how does it go?"
"how does the love song of the insane go?"
"that one, yes"
so I lean against the wall into her
and I open my mouth
very slowly
and I begin to sing.

Edge

did nothing today
stayed away from everyone
sharpened my love for you
from a dull knife
into an impossible edge
that can slice unripe fruit
meat, bone and brick
anything, really
come closer
I want to show you.

Acknowledgements

Thank you, Spout, Heather Dorn, Matthew Guerruckey, Andrew Feindt, Shali Nicolas, William Seward Bonnie, Misti Rainwater-Lites, Dustin Holland, Kevin Ridgeway, Frank Reardon, Robert Vaughan, Amanda Deo, Michele McDannold, Erin Lynn, Mark Brunetti, James Duncan and Allan Ferguson. Last but not least, major thanks to Gary and Robin Smith, for surrounding me with books, music and art, and never faltering with the love. Muchas gracias.

I am grateful for the support and guidance of the editors and publishers of the magazines, anthologies, and websites where portions of this book have already appeared: *Olentangy Review*, *The Nervous Breakdown*, *Citizens for Decent Literature*, *Full of Crow*, *Thunderclap!*, *Clutching at Straws*, *Zygote in My Coffee*, *Santa Fe Literary Review*, and *The Idiom Magazine*.

Bud Smith lives in Washington Heights, NYC, but is originally from New Jersey, right there by the ocean. He's the author of the novel *Tollbooth*, and the short story collection *Or Something Like That*. Most of the things he owns he found at the flea market for about a dollar.

WWW.BUDSMITHWRITES.COM

The 31st is coming
and with it the sky will gray, confort
confuse sunrises with sunsets.
All the open cans of soda in
the alleys will begin to rattle
as my fingernails brittle snap
and I have nightmares of
doorknobs with eyes white
as peroxide clouds.

You would not condone my
Chrysler, but would look around
for the chassises lazy flipped over
like broken armadillows.
If you could come back, imagine
your dismay at my Njen chamber,
at the bamboo shutes that always
seem to flower and grow regardless
of water. Chinese warlords used
those to torture people you know?
I heard they used to put
the slivers under people's fingernails
you'd say. What if I told you
about your sister's divorce, revealed
who really put
the hammer into
the drywall
like a knife to ivory